# Bigger Than The Sky

## *Praise for* Bigger Than The Sky

What a lovely, refreshing, honest expression of non-duality! With humility and compassion, Vicki speaks to the Knowing in all of us, reminding us of the possibility of finding grace and gratitude in even the darkest parts of our lives. A delightful and moving book of love and loss, seeking and discovery, pain and surrender. Highly recommended!

**Jeff Foster, author of *The Deepest Acceptance* and *Falling in Love With Where You Are*.**

I thought I was done with books, but this one is free of the spiritual ego that taints so much writing. It is refreshing, with an intimacy that is seamless and honest.

**John Troy, author of *Wisdom's Soft Whisper***

This is a really powerful book; a delicate and artful balance between transcendence and humanity. I love the way it flows… connected by a thematic thread yet non-linear. I am finding it an inspirational and very fluid read.

Reading this book is like sitting under a waterfall; Vicki's words wash over you in a most purifying and heart-opening way.

**David Newman, author of *The Timebound Traveler***

For her newest book *Bigger than the Sky*, Vicki Woodyard has selected the perfect title. Unlike so many books on offer today that only present the author's own expression of what they consider the truth, this one moves between two similar but somewhat different points of understanding, giving the reader a view of a VERY BIG SKY indeed. As we move between Vicki's words and the words of her friend Peter, limiting beliefs of what one thought was true can dissolve. I highly recommend this book for anyone ready to stop thinking "I already know" to experiencing something far bigger.

**Mary Margaret Moore, author of *I Come As A Brother: The Teachings of Bartholomew***

This book is an ongoing "steady gaze into what is," as Vicki points out in her characteristically human way. Vicki has a rare gift in being able to take spiritual awakening out of its esoteric sheath and bring it into the everyday heart of human life, with all its ups, downs, beauty and ugliness. Having been diagnosed and then freed of cancer, I found her essays about her husband Bob's cancer so poignant and right on target. Everything in life is a gift, even death and cancer, as this book points out. As Vicki writes, we come to see the living experience of ourselves, no adjectives needed. Enjoy these little essay gems!

**Scott Kiloby, author of *Living Relationship: Finding Harmony With Others***

# Bigger Than The Sky
## A Radical Awakening

Vicki Woodyard

NON-DUALITY PRESS

NON-DUALITY PRESS | PO Box 2228 | Salisbury | SP2 2GZ
United Kingdom

ISBN: 978-1-908664-45-7

www.non-dualitypress.org

# TABLE OF CONTENTS

# FOREWORD

Vicki Woodyard's writing is about reality. She reveals the place beyond pain and suffering by being factual and direct, by looking straight at suffering. The magic of her writing is directness, humor, and artistry exacting a sweetness that transcends suffering.

How does Vicki achieve this? In this book it is by way of a literary relationship with Peter. Now Peter's a whole other influence in my life. I didn't know Peter personally, but his website, sentient.org, inspired me to start nonduality.com.

Sentient.org was dedicated to Ramana Maharshi and consisted of a collection of writings from enlightened sages living and deceased. So here's what we have in this book. Two people facing every shape and shadow of sorrow. Two people seeing through sorrow, seeing what is real. Peter and Vicki emerge as a pair for the ages. We join them because we all know pain. We are Vicki. And Peter. And Laurie, Bob, Bessie, Vernon Howard, and three cats and a pup that gets put down too. Oy. At some point you have to laugh at it all. You have to see what really matters. Peter and Vicki do. I did. You will.

That's what this book is: community. Like the old Nonduality Salon, it's a community in which you're not safe. Sorry about that. You have to face pain and sorrow. There's nothing to protect you here. How else to realize what Vicki confesses: "In one sense, sorrow

is the true guru, and when it burns away the dross of
the self, only holy ash remains."

*Jerry Katz*

FOR PETER

I will meet you out beyond the breaking
but how will I know you?
For you have disappeared into your life
and come out no one, ho ho.
Perhaps a memory of you
will light the blueness of the sky
and I will recognize the taste of
conversation we once had and
then we disappeared into the fire.

## Note to the Reader

The essays that make up this book are not in strict chronological order. They are more in *kyros* (God's) time than *chronos* (clock and calendar) time. What I hope is clear is how Peter and I flowed together through a dark tunnel of time. As a result, this book was written.

Some of these essays appeared in *Life With A Hole In It: That's How The Light Gets In*.

*Vicki Woodyard*

# Peter

In a time of overwhelm, a man named Peter befriended me online. He had founded sentient.org, one of the earliest spiritual sites. He never gave his last name or where he lived. The facts about Peter are few; he preferred it that way.

Little did I know that Peter's words, so simple at the time, would continue to bear fruit for me and others. I do not know when Peter died. He just grew weaker and less able to compose emails to me and his other friends.

Now his light emanates from these pages. Welcome to the story of Peter and me.

# How It Began

When my husband was dying, I began an email correspondence with a man named Peter who was ill from a series of strokes. He could barely get around and yet he told me he was "bigger than the sky." After his strokes, he found that the old pile of adjectives around him did him no good. "I am a good-looking man, a man's man," he told me once. And yet he found himself unable to walk down the hall to the bathroom for two years running. The new adjectives people were using were not particularly helpful. Strings of words like "poor prognosis, stroke victim, unable to work" were now applied to him.

Peter was barely holding onto life and my husband was dying. Neither Peter nor I had time to waste on concepts. Although we had both been on the Way for a long time, now we jettisoned any deep thoughts in exchange for the chance to hang out in the rarefied air of simplicity.

Peter had been to spiritual teachers and found them to be useless. "They could not help me," he said. "They simply did not know how." So he did the only thing he was able to do. He sat in the sunshine with a little cat named Alex on his chest. The cat's purrs, in lieu of a nursing staff, conveyed to him the healing power of nature. He watched the robins run across the grass because they were what he saw. He was grateful in the most basic way. And he began to realize that what he had found was the living experience of himself. No adjectives need apply.

And so I sat in my leather recliner in perfectly good health, and remembered that I too was not who I thought or felt I was. I simply *was*.

By the end of the morning I had a wastebasket full of words that seemed to describe me. I was bigger than any of them. I knew what Peter knew—that I was bigger than the sky. I was bigger than anything that could be named or described. Peter is no longer among us and yet he lives within all who loved him. How does he do this? I was never sure how Peter did anything but feel the joy of the moment. "When I am in pain, I yell. And when I fall down, I say 'ho ho'." But he never latched onto anything. His own sense of *I am* became stronger than any stroke could ever be.

Once he had a brilliant career and then, after the strokes, he had almost no memory of who he was or who his friends were. He couldn't make change. But he sure made a difference. You see, the *I am* that we all are is indestructible. It is too bad we don't learn this unless we are reduced to helplessness. In Peter's case, he saw through the illusion of having a separate self. He realized that no matter where he found himself, he was bigger. And that brought him joy that few of us will ever know.

We were both living the bare bones of a life. His physical capabilities limited by a series of strokes, he managed to leave me with a record of reality that survives only on love. Putting dogma aside, he reveled in the simplicity of each breath, each faltering step.

If I had to sum up what Peter meant to me, I would say that he offered me himself. And that was so powerful as to render me ripped open. The inner became the outer and vice versa. He treated me to stories of his cats; and I, in return, swapped tales of how it felt to be in charge of someone who was dying. You'd think these exchanges would have been sad, but they weren't. They were fashioned of something as fine as the ether, as indescribable as air and as necessary.

"For what it's worth, I hold your hand in this," he said, and every time I read the words of my gentle friend, his far-reaching wisdom, sprinkled with laughter, carries me back home to the heart.

When I take a walk around my neighborhood, I often see the robins running across the grass. My heart opens to the understanding that Peter gave me. I am bigger than anything I see. I am bigger than the sky.

# Where Do I Stand?

*One of the absolute qualifications for a writer is not knowing his arse from his elbow.*

Leonard Cohen

My editor asked me: What do you mean by spirit, what do you mean by soul?

I replied with a quote:

*Who looks out with my eyes? What is the soul? I cannot stop asking.* ~ Rumi

Our questions should be carried for a lifetime. We should live them carefully, as if God Himself were listening.

Writers, and poets in particular, know how to encode these questions in order to help them live. For example, this whole book is about soul, or spirit. For Peter realized that his very nature was love. For me, awareness and love are one and the same thing.

I listened to Peter as he spoke to me from in-between the lines. When he described himself as being bigger than the sky, that was not to be taken literally. It was a soul knowing that he shared with many people. I was not the only one that benefited from his awakening.

If my writing does anything, it opens the reader to a softer place than words can reach. I use words to go beyond words. But doesn't every good writer do that? I hope so.

As far as my speaking to Bob as if he were alive and he could hear me, who can disprove that? It is the natural human response to loss. After someone dies, we carry that love to a higher level and there we plant it for higher purposes. What grows is the eternal side of love. Yes, there are tears involved. They soften the ground for that flower of love to be planted. And so we gather courage to go on without their physical presence. Peter is no longer on this earth, but his spirit is hanging around...

# Who Are We Then?

I sat watching the body of my daughter lying in the small coffin.
It wasn't her.
I lay awake at night mourning.
It wasn't me.
My son turned inward.
It wasn't him.
My husband fell silent.
It wasn't him.
Who was it?

I sat and wrote about my daughter.
It wasn't me.
My husband became a workaholic.
It wasn't him.
Our son grew distant.
It wasn't him.

My husband grew ill.
It wasn't him.
I was angry.
It wasn't me.
I sat watching the body of my husband lying in his coffin.
It wasn't him.
My son and I were strong for each other.
It wasn't us.

Who are we when the chips are down
and the shit has hit the proverbial fan?
It isn't us.

Who are we when, like angels, we soar into
the impossible with great dignity? It isn't us.
Who are we when, like mighty fortresses,
we stand against the darkness?
It isn't us.

Who am I? Who are we when we love
and fail to feel anything but devastation?
Who are we when we numb out and
retreat into the fortress of the mind.
Who rolls away the stone of grief
and says, "Come out, the light will no longer be
denied."
Who are we then? Who are we?

# A Conversation with Peter

*Most of the time I just try to rest and play with my gentle little cat in the sunlight. Nothing else is important.*

Peter

The things that Peter said carried great resonance for me and, with his permission, I am sharing some of our dialogue below.

*Peter:* This life of ours is so short—an eye blink and it is gone. I think it is very lovely that you and your husband could hold hands together even while walking through hell. Who knows what may come? In joy or in suffering, this amazing life dazzles us all.

*Vicki:* You sound as if you might be ill yourself.

*Peter:* That's what my doctors say. I don't believe them. My little cat never gives tomorrow or yesterday a thought. Sometimes she hurts and asks for comfort. Sometimes she is tired and lies gently in the warm sun smiling up at me. What more could there be? No wonder Ramana Maharshi loved Lakshmi (his favorite cow) so very much. Lakshmi and my little cat are not going anywhere. They never have. How blessed.

Rest is greatly undervalued. It seems to me that most people in this society have not had genuine rest since they were young children. No wonder there is such unhappiness. I feel that most of the folks sitting in satsangs are really just looking for a little rest. Animals are so much smarter. They rest when they are tired. Now there's a sensible life!

It is my own experience that pain is something of an eye-opener. Pain that goes on for years tends to drown out the silliness of belief systems in favor of direct contact with life, God, or whatever one wishes to call truth.

Intermediaries are a waste of time when the body is crumbling. I have found that such difficulties tend to make all other sounds meaningless. Only the beating of one's own true heart has meaning.

*Vicki:* Right after Bob was diagnosed, I wrote to Pamela Wilson; I clung to these words of hers in my sadness and uncertainty. "Rest and rapture, what else is there?" she said.

*Peter:* The person that Pamela says was her teacher (Robert Adams) took a long, slow time in dying of Parkinson's disease. I met him about a year before the end. He could barely speak and shook constantly, but his inner peace and beauty shone like a beacon. Even in the middle of a failing body he rested deeply within himself. Very lovely.

It is my own experience that suffering is what most of us do best. And much of that suffering is a result of trying to fend off strong feelings. It is my experience that nothing works anyway. In really serious illness there often is no way out. So why not do the only thing left open, which is to rest and enjoy the light sparkling on the trees? There really is nothing else. You will think I've lost it, but for me the aloneness has become a very lovely thing. I do not feel alone, as in isolated or cut off. Rather this aloneness is in a sense a powerlessness, which is very peaceful. There really is nothing I or anyone can do, so I may as well smile with my little cat in my arms and live as best I can.

As I type, that cat is asking for dinner. She is really good at being present at all times, especially at dinnertime. I think she has more wisdom in her little finger than 99.999% of all the so-called teachers out there. And talk about good-looking! Only Ramana had a face as lovely as hers.

Illness (and anything else for that matter) is beyond my or anyone's control. *Sigh*, I'm not very good with words. I think I'm trying to say that I have found that planning and worrying (which the mind is designed to do) go on, of course. But so what. My mind may continue to suffer, but that's not me, so let it suffer if it wants to. It is none of my concern. There is nothing it can do anyway.

*Vicki:* I understand how little energy you have. If I had any choice about the matter, I would just stop everything and be like your beloved cat.

*Peter:* I feel my friend the cat has more competence as a healer than all of these others combined. Not to mention infinitely more compassion.

*Vicki*: Gurus can be just as bad as doctors.

*Peter:* Yes. Why anyone would want to teach (as opposed to sharing) is a mystery to me. I feel that sometimes someone has an experience and thinks he is special, so he puts up a sign and advertises his services. The desperate and the frightened come, invest heavily, and eventually end up with an experience of their own, and then put up their own sign on the street. Invisible prison walls.

It has been many years since I felt a difference between guru and student, or awakened and unawakened. It is my experience that such terms have no meaning, serving only to get in the way of time spent lying in the warm sunlight with a cat in one's arms.

*My note on this:* God speaks to us in varied ways, including cats and sunlight and newfound friends. The only thing to do is listen.

# Bare

Two meteors crashed through my life, leaving it the way it looks today: bare—consciously bare.

The first meteor was my youngest child's diagnosis of a fatal cancer. She was treated at St. Jude Children's Research Hospital for two years and spent the last year of her life in remission. The cancer had spread to her lungs and she was given a course of radiation. Her doctor said to us, "This will give her six months to a year and then the cancer will return." She died on a hot July morning right after she turned seven.

My husband and I and our son Rob—dear Rob, who was only ten years old when his sister died—soldiered on. My husband immersed himself in work—a default option for many men after a loss. I was trying to live a normal life—what a joke! People looked on our family as pariahs; death shouldn't happen to a first grader—and yet it had. All they knew to do was look the other way.

So I took my first steps on the spiritual path. I read many books, beginning with Yogananda's classic, *The Autobiography of a Yogi*, and I liked the writings of Joel Goldsmith, the founder of "The Infinite Way." It would take me many years to even begin to live a true teaching. My darkness was considerable, but I was doing all I could to stumble into light.

I was led to a great spiritual teacher, Vernon Howard. Bob and I would often fly to Las Vegas and then drive for an hour and a half to Boulder City,

Nevada, to hear him speak. Powerful synchronicities guided me. The darkness of my life was made even darker by Mr. Howard, for he was a genius at bringing subconscious suffering to light. He offered no quick fixes; only a steady beam of light aimed into our darkness.

That darkness is our way of thinking and mechanical way of being. The goal is conscious living and as Vernon Howard said, "No man knowingly hurts himself." Since all we do is hurt ourselves, the inference is that we are sleepwalking our way through life. Jesus knew this, when He said, "Forgive them, Father. They know not what they do."

Twenty years or so passed and then one day Bob began to look pale and tired all the time. It was months before he was told the reason. He had multiple myeloma—a cancer of the bone marrow. I was devastated. The man who had given me strength when our daughter died was leaving me just like she had.

I wasn't ready to give up another love, but I had no choice. They had the same prognosis: a terminal cancer with about three years to live. She died right on schedule; he eked out an extra year and a half. That was partly thanks to me, who saw to it that he didn't miss a meal. But I paid the price. All of what I saw as my spiritual progress now took giant backward lurches. At the end of his illness I was mean and tired. I believe that is technically called burnout. It doesn't matter what it is called. It is the dark night of the soul. But I never stopped believing in the light.

## Life Is a Ballet

Life is a ballet and, although it looks and feels beautiful at times, our toes are bleeding and we wake in the night with muscle cramps. All of this strenuous effort creates beauty that is our reward.

I have never danced as hard as when my small daughter was fighting cancer. She, herself, took ballet at the age of five although she had a large muscle missing from her right leg. It contained the tumor that had to be removed. I had to stand on the sidelines and grimace as she tried to do what the healthy little girls were doing. She was thin as a rail and white as a sheet, but she persevered because what little girl doesn't love ballet?

It was a dance of love for her, trying to give her a 'normal' life until she died. It was well worth it. Our Swan Lake was the real thing and, when all of the curtain calls had been taken, she never returned.

Many years have gone by since her death and I am still writing about it. I have let go of her but the lessons learned are still bearing fruit. I have learned to trust beauty, whether it is of the heart, body or soul. It is truth in motion and it requires immense effort to create what looks like effortless beauty.

I have no doubt but that the ballet of life has a master choreographer. Someone who knows who is wearing the new tutus and pink slippers; someone who trusts that the music will be sweet and that the slippers have enough resin applied before the performance.

I never see Swan Lake without being moved. The real can never be taken from us, but the illusion is poignant indeed. Every year there are new dancers in the cast and in the beginning it seems that nothing will come together at the right time.

Certainly as I danced through my daughter's life with cancer over a period of three years, I often sat on the floor and wept, but I always got back up and played my part. I followed the doctor's instructions to give her a normal life. That included her dancing, wincing and triumphing. Her dance teacher, of course, fell in love with her, as did all who came to know her brave spirit. Love knows the steps that it must take in the ballet of life.

# The Great Physician

In the midst of suffering and serious illness, we are often deluged by the demands that are suddenly thrust upon us. It doesn't matter that friends and family are rallying round. We need something that is beyond the human capacity to give. We sense the lack. We utter prayers in utter isolation. Where is hope... where is true help and healing?

I remember a night in the hospital when my husband was still quite ill after his diagnosis of multiple myeloma. We were wrestling with God about how He could inflict such sorrow on us -yet again. Our only daughter had died of a rare childhood cancer when she was seven years old. My husband, son and I had lived with the desolation for many years, for no one ever gets over the death of a child or a sibling.

This night we were devastatingly alone. I had called two agencies putting in a request. But evidently the nurse that they called did not receive the message in time, and she entered the room quietly. She wore a colorful knit hat on her head and the sweetest smile that we had ever seen. She seemed totally intent on what she had come to do, which wasn't to provide a traditional nursing service. Oh, no!

We explained to her that she wasn't needed, as the nurse from the other agency was on the way. But the three of us all knew better. This was far beyond human scheduling. Bessie, as her name turned out to be, told us her story. She said that she had come all the way across town… she might as well stay and visit for a bit. She is a nurse, but she is also a believer. She said she tried to tell her story to one person a day—her story of a living God. Bob and I held hands as I stood by his bed. His arm was full of gizmos and contraptions. We both wept like children and were comforted by her words. She read from the Bible and loved us in a heartfelt way.

Peace pervaded that room. It was a cloak of comfort that she offered. Sitting down in the old cracked Naugahyde chair, she read passages from the Bible and warned us against fear getting a foothold. Three against the flood of fear… two of us fearing that the waters would overwhelm us. Bessie Owens left her business card along with her healing presence when she gathered up her pocketbook and her prayers. She didn't fool me for a minute. When she left I knew that the Great Physician had been making His rounds.

## Love Between the Lines

I love my first book, *Life With A Hole In It*. This morning I drank a cup of tea and reread it for the umpteenth time. It speaks to me of love between the lines, between health and sickness, between tears and laughter. I lived much of it between the cracks, feeling stuff that was indecipherable in words.

My tall, strong husband became my child towards the end of his illness. I, who had been a Southern belle of sorts, now became a preview of coming attractions, a steel magnolia in the making. I, who had been a diligent spiritual student, now became the path itself. No choice in any of this, I might add. It was a grueling, choiceless experience.

These days I am enjoying "having written." Deep within my soul I am sprouting hope and joy, something I went without in those other days, like a camel in the desert. These seeds will bear fruit in time. All I have to do is let the light shine. And between the rows of hope and joy, I wander down the page. I turn them one at a time, savoring the connection I have now made with readers. They know me like the back of their hand, because my story is theirs as well. It was an arduous journey, one made in heartache and futility. Letting go was not an option; it was written in the stars. Now they wink again with light.

After I wrote *Life With A Hole In It*, I didn't know what would happen as a result of publishing it. But it has been accepted and even embraced. For me, that is a miracle, since I revealed myself warts and all. Now there is seemingly nothing left to say.

Let me explain what I mean by that. At the end of that book, there is an essay in which I express my grief and its accompanying feelings of *How could a loving God do this to me?* And then a silence falls upon the page. The reader understands that the story has been told. Now what?

*Now what?* is everyone's question who has ever put their feet on the upward way. That question is a book in itself. What do you do when there is nothing to do but accept the way things are? A good *koan* to ponder. I hope the ending of the book is one answer to that question. I have read it many times over. Each time I see something new in it. Being the author, that seems to be a dumb thing to say. That just tells me it is going to be around for a while. I worry about how to find its audience when it knows better than I do. Life is strange; mystery works better than fact sometimes.

# My Place in the Inner World

I write about the hard stuff because it is so familiar to me. Once you have buried a child, your life changes forever. There is no return to the garden unless you choose to awaken right here and now. My daughter's name was Laurie and she looked like an angel. Long brown hair and mischievous eyes. Screaming in terror when her number came up in the chemo room. Vomiting all night from it. Crying because she was always sick. Laughing as she told us riddles. She was my wakeup call.

She died before finishing the last bottle of root beer in her room at a children's hospital. She smelled like pee and her beloved yellow blanket. She was seven years old plus five weeks. So she was buried in her birthday dress with the wrist corsage a kind person sent for her to wear in her casket. I made it through the first five years after her death. They were the hardest. Recovering from the loss of a child is slow. The only friend you have is... yourself, because no one else wants to be around you. You remind them of the charnel house—an old-fashioned word these days. *I smelled of death.*

Our whole family smelled of it. We breathed it in and out. We ate our meals and gamely took the first vacation where I burst into tears in some seafood restaurant before the entree arrived. At home, I yelled at my son and he retreated into his private emotional hell. Bob buried himself in work. And life went on because it must and should. But we were not thrilled.

And that was over thirty years ago. Why don't I shut up already? Because long ago I remember reading an old-fashioned poem written by a man who had buried his young daughter. This is an age-old subject that brings people to their knees. While I was down there on mine, I decided to pray. It did little good but I kept my hand in at it. I also read libraries of self-help books. I found a teacher and gave myself over to inner work. I had found my place in the inner world at least.

# An Invitation to Rest

*One should rest when it is time to rest and act
when it is time to act. True resting and putting
to rest are attained through the disappearance
of the ego, which leads to the harmony of one's
behavior with the laws of the universe. Resting
in principle involves doing that which is right in
every position in which one is placed.*

I Ching (B.C. 1150?)

I heard from Peter, today. After a long absence due
to continued illness, he writes—with that remarkable
lucidity of his:

"The sky still sparkles and the cats still dance
through the grasses. Deer come and nuzzle the roses.
In everything there is a quiet vibrancy. I watch the
birds in the trees—lovers at the kiss of the sky. What
else is there?"

Peter says that there is nothing that you can do
to obtain grace. It either happens or it doesn't. That
is believable coming from him. It is as if he is saying,
*Relax*!

Peter is not physically well and doesn't have a lot
of energy, yet he has been there for me, a stranger,
in a way that is unfathomable. Perhaps you can feel
his energy, too. It is an energy that twinkles as he
speaks of a beloved cat with whom he hangs out. It
is also an energy that simply tells the truth—about
living with pain, about sitting in the sun, about being

one with what is. Perhaps this is a familiar philosophy to you—that resting in God, resting within, can do wonders to restore the soul. Most of us become too busy to bother with such simple strength. I invite you to rest with Peter and me.

## Bigger than the Sky

Peter has an uncanny ability to bypass the mind. Anything he says is total. He allows emotions to come and go, passing across the sky of his being. A laugh, a tear—all the same to him.

Clearly more intelligent than many of us, Peter has been challenged by an illness that has left him with little energy. For those of us who have been privileged to communicate with him, this makes him even dearer. His self-deprecatory emails to me are priceless.

When I told him that, if I lived near him, I would come over to borrow a cup of enlightenment, he just said that he didn't know anything about it, wasn't interested in it and had none to give. Yeah, right.

Peter is so candid about the frailty of his body. Yet he follows these confessions of weakness with such empathy for the universe that you want to reach out and hug him. But he seems to be nowhere and everywhere.

Peter calls himself a cat-juggler. When he speaks of sitting in the sun with his cat, he is speaking about all of us learning how to let go. I know little about the details of Peter's life. They seem not to matter to him anymore.

I suspect that talking to Peter gives one a contact high. Just what is it that he has learned through suffering? How does he transmit such wisdom in so few words? I know what he is up to. He is involving me in the paradox of peace. Shame on him! He is showing me surrender. How dare he? He is chiding me for clinging to the body. I might have known. Peter is loving me by letting me go.

## Losing Interest in your Story

I was talking with Peter recently about the fact that he had lost interest in his story. That is what makes him so lovable. The most he would say is that he woke up one day and his "me" was gone.

Those of us who still believe in our personal story —the biographical details that we cobble together to make the "me"—will continue to suffer emotionally. Joel Goldsmith healed by sitting down and turning away from the problems of his clients. So did many other healers. So I ask you, would you rather be lovable or would you rather cling to your personal story?

Peter exemplifies love, so loss of interest in the personal story can lead to deeper love. Alienation from the self often occurs precisely because we are too interested in our story. We have two choices. We can turn within and enter the silence or we can consciously turn toward life and its ongoing renewal.

My story lately has not been a pretty one, but then I am not alone in this. And there are many people who would clamor to tell me theirs. Yet if I turn away from it, lose interest in it, let the details of it atrophy, love will occupy the vacuum. Simple as that.

Peter always tells me about just sitting in the sunshine with his cat and letting her love him. There is no story going on, just this moment of pure peace. I defy you not to love a man like Peter.

# The Wind on Your Skin

Peter always lets me know that to feel the wind on your skin is a blessed thing. Forget illness, sorrow, unsolvable human problems. He has known more than his share and carries his burden so gracefully. I have never met Peter but I don't have to. He is a pointer to the real just as much as Ramana Maharshi or Nisargadatta Maharaj. The twinkle in his eye is a universal one. How blessed we are by people like Peter. How can you find him? You got me. I feel his love in every honest word that he writes....

"The only thing I have ever found that really works (for me at least) is just being. By which I mean sitting or walking through the grasses, not doing anything much, feeling the air and the sun, seeing the wide, wide sky, and just poking along. For me, what helps when pain comes is to scream as appropriate, then go on with the walk (or crawl depending on strength) through the grass.

Talk of enlightenment, it seems to me, is for the healthy only, since they think that by hard work and strict discipline they can attain something. For those of us who are seriously ill however, all that seems like impossibly hard work. 'Enlightenment', 'awakening', and the like seems to me to be all just a lot of talk and hard work—really just a way of avoiding the wind in one's hair, so easily available anywhere at any time, regardless of circumstance, without any effort at all. Trying to attain something more seems, well, uninteresting."

# An Awakened Man

You know you are writing about an awakened man when the fingers at the keyboard will only type the correct words. If I try and paint an inauthentic picture of Peter, I will be unable to see it into print. I did not experience his physicality but his transcendence. And thereby hangs a tale.

For when someone has been shattered, bereft of the ordinary human ways of navigating the world, what and who they are will manifest immediately. The shell will crack and fall away, leaving us with the meat of the character.

I did not so much as meet Peter but recognize him by his sheer simplicity. You can read his words again and again and never fail to feel renewed. The timeless world was his. In it, cats lolled upon his chest, robins scurried across his lawn and he hollered "ho ho" at it all. It was one huge joke to Peter. A doctor was a joke; a guru was a joke; his condition was a joke. He shared this with me, but also with many others. I can only say that his impact was enormous.

I gave him my heart, which was so very easy. He gave me his, as well as his hand in friendship. He knew that I was filled to the brim with suffering; he had a way of emptying the cup so that we could simply talk. So we talked about Bob's journey through cancer and his own—through various and sundry disabilities. He had disabling migraines and quite a few trips to the hospital as the emails traveled between us.

When he returned from a hospital visit, he always had plenty to say - none of it good. He would report on how they prodded his helpless limbs and said dire things about his future. For him, doctors were quite useless; they had not one whit of power to heal him. This he knew. He was not bitter; he simply experienced his actual state.

"My wife tells me that I have aged," he reported in one email. "My beard is quite white now, but I am still a handsome guy. Ho ho!" He didn't give a rap about his reputation. He had nothing to lose. And his way of being was that of a child who has discovered that he can play and nap whenever he likes. What a life....

## Faltering Steps

Our friendship was a rope running from my computer to his. We did not discuss spirituality all that much. I would give him reports from the front, about sitting all day in the chemo room with Bob. He would talk of resting and watching robins run. Between us there was such gentle humor. His simplicity untangled my knotted-up heart. I could rest with him.

I was honing my skills as a writer while my heart was breaking and my body was exhausted. Writing was deep solace for me. For Peter, it required extraordinary self-discipline to complete an email. He would frequently write, "Got to stop and rest now." Through his honest admission of fatigue, he gave me permission to rest my own mind and heart.

His cats were his world; I still find that amazing. Although he clearly loved his wife, he never said much about her. Instead he taught me how he saw life. He lived it among his cats and nature. He got down on their level and let them be his teachers. He roamed the yard with them. He sat and let himself be their furniture. And I would write about how my life was falling apart. His had fallen together.

We both faced grim futures. His would end in one last breath. Mine in the death of my beloved spouse. We were good soldiers, albeit weary ones. His light allowed me to take one step further into the darkness of watching someone die.

Peter's wife and my husband were our beloveds,

but we needed space in which to give full attention to ourselves for a bit of time. I never thought of Peter as benefiting from the conversations we had. He was so wise.

When I asked him if he would consider writing a book with me, he said, "Funny, a lot of people are asking me that, but I simply am not well enough." And so now, years down the road, he joins me once again on the screen of my Mac. The beloved cannot leave; the beloved is revealed as the eternal Self that we are. Ultimately, we are all dancing in the dark, doing the best we can with what we have. Peter's steps were faltering ones, but somehow that was exactly what I needed.

# A Message to Peter

*Vicki:* Peter, you have the uncanny ability to open my heart and I have never met you. I am sure that I am not the first person to tell you this. Ever since you first told me about sitting in the sun with your cat, I have been enchanted by such a simple teaching—given so effortlessly. Since you have been challenged by adversity, this is not true. This kind of effortless-ness is embedded in super effort. I know you say that grace either happens or it doesn't and I tend to agree with you. But if I tell you that you are gracing me, you will deny it.

Nevertheless... every time I hear from you, my heart opens like a door into the place that I really live. It is warm and spacious and caring. Irony can breathe here, but it is mostly gentle. Wit with wis-dom, warmth with candor.

You say that you are moving, but where would you go? I think that someone like Ramana said this... and I hope that it is true... that you are totally here and now, always. It is my hope that you will let me share some of your insights with others. Most of us are still living with a closed heart, with a sense that the "me" is fragile and filled with suffering. Talking to you is to open the heart, trusting that the space left open will be occupied by ease.

I hope that you know I mean business. This is not an idle whim, but an inner certainty that you have something to share as easily as your cat does when she

is sunning herself with you. So let me hear from you...
may I let some people listen in on our conversations?

    Always, Vicki

## Nothing to Cling to

Dear Vicki,

I went through a hell that was horrible when I first started to get so seriously ill. I lost a lot of things. Career, friends, health, loves, ability to read, and … well, more than most folks can ever imagine in their worst dreams. The hospital had said there was no hope of recovery, ever.

Turning to spirituality, philosophy, learning, advaita, non-dualism and so forth did not help in any way. Turning to people who said they were awake was a joke—I found nothing there that was helpful or even particularly compassionate. I did discover one small thing that seemed to help a little: as much as possible I did my darnedest to not look to the past or the future. As the losses and suffering started to mount up, I did this with more and more intensity. And then even more… one day something died. I do not know how to say it, other than to say I no longer had a sense of a "me" at the center of things anymore, or anywhere else for that matter….

I am not sure why I am writing this to you now, or if my own experience can be of any help at all, or if it just sounds silly or a tad flakey? Yet it does seem that there is an intensity that can happen sometimes which shows us so very clearly, and yes, sometimes painfully, that there is nothing to cling to any more ….

Peter

# Breaking

Inwardly I was breaking up—or was I breaking down? Outwardly I was shaking, trying to hold everything in place. It felt like planets were falling from the sky and I was either dodging them or trying to hold them up. It was a miserable, miserable descent into hell. All of the teachings flew in my face and mocked me, or so it seemed.

I had been raised to be a good little girl and I did my best to keep up the facade. *Your husband is dying. Be a good little wife. Go with him to the doctor, take over the jobs he used to do, continue to maintain a good home and never let 'em see you sweat.* I didn't.

Writing soon became my salvation. I knew how to write. I did not know how to watch a fatal disease unfold in front of my eyes and then sleep in my bed every night. For I was nurse as well as wife. Towards the end he was my child and I was his parent. But I could write.

I was an embedded reporter from the chemo room. I sat patiently there for hours while Bob was hooked up to an IV. I loved the courage of the patients and their families. I realized I was more practical than I gave myself credit for. The only thing that really stymied me was driving. Some days I would have to let Bob off on the ground floor and then try and find a parking spot in a crowded garage. One time I just couldn't remember where I left the car and the security guard had to put us in his van and drive us around until I said "Oh, there it is." And yet I was a force of nature seven days a week. Of course I was exhausted. In my despair one day I cried out to Bob, "You would never take as good care of me as I am taking of you!" It was the truth but it was coming from a very dark place. I was losing myself as well as losing him.

I stood by him and wrote. I watched him be valiant. I listened to his stories of childhood because he needed to sum up his life. So we sat at the kitchen table and talked, while our son listened with a breaking heart.

Today I had an earth-shaking cry. It did me so much good. I cried for every moment of those five years. I cried for the hard ways in which I have learned my lessons. Yesterday a plumber treated me like a nutcase for telling him he had installed my bath tub faucets backwards. That is what brought on the tears. A jerk—but he led me to the place I needed to go.

I know how to write. I know how to express things in an intuitive straightforward way. I am not sure I know how to love myself. That is the last lesson and the hardest.

# ICU

*Vicki*: Bob was in ICU and has been in the hospital for a week.

*Peter:* Oh Vicki. I am so sorry that this has appeared. The ICU is no fun at all.

*Vicki:* I am weeping copiously… out of control.

*Peter*: Well, this is certainly understandable. Fear is seldom easy. My wife has spent some time crying too. Last night we watched a comedy show together and she laughed a lot, which made me laugh too, which started the cats off and Maple and Alexandra and Sandra snarled at them and a generally good time was had by all.

*Vicki:* This joy you experience—I am unfamiliar with it.

*Peter:* I have attached a small mp3 file which I made for you today of me playing a toy flute. It's got lots of mistakes as one hand seems to not work as well as it used to when doing the fingering plus I tend to lose my breath, but hopefully you will enjoy anyway.

Today too I had some trouble staying upright, scaring my wife, ho ho! But trying to change the changeless seems like a lot of work, so I look at the trees and the sunlight, and smile and grab for a nearby wall, ho ho!

I watch Alex run and tumble with her brother... there is a fullness and an ease so wonderful and so joyous. I wish with all my heart that Bob were not ill. Ah Vicki, we savor this breath in all its beauty. Who knows what will come next...?

# Peter and the Cat

As long as I emailed Peter, his cats were the topic of much of his conversation. He spoke of Alex, the black and white cat, the most. She it was who lay on his chest and purred to him of impermanence, you might say.

I had told him Bob was doing better and this is his reply:

"This is good news indeed. I hope that he continues to do so. This life seems to be touch and go from moment to moment. It is my own experience that pain, whether psychological, physiological or whatever, is very fleeting unless constantly recreated. I watch the robins pulling worms out of the safe warm earth so that their nestlings can fly high and strong, even as the cats stalk them for dinner. Perhaps the only permanence is in the gentle quiet in which it all appears to happen."

I say, "My writing has been going unusually well." He replies, "I think a book would be a lovely thing, and of great help. I have a feeling that you may wonder about an ego rising for a while during the process? It seems to me that no matter how sweet ego or imagination may be, nothing sticks to the sky in which they appear. Perhaps that which is not what one is, cannot stick to what one is. So whether an ego appears to rise or not, may be in fact of no import at all."

At another time Peter said, "When I was young I lived in a parking lot. Finding ways to avoid freezing to death at night was an adventure. Finding food was sometimes fun, too. I met people that most people in this society ignore, and who had little chance of finding help—when illness took them they were done. I feel that who made it and who did not did not depend at all upon who they were inside. The idea that an idea could have saved one and not another seems to me to be an idea!"

# Peter's Birthday

This is Peter's reply to my wish for a happy birthday.

"Thank you! The rumor of birth is an odd one. How we cherish the experience that we were born, have grown up, and are now somehow the result of all that.

Little Maple (the universe's most perfect being) moves more slowly than I seem to remember, but he tells me that he is ageless. This makes sense to me, as his eyes are brighter than the sun."

*Vicki:* I wish you hadn't gone and gotten sick.

*Peter:* Lots of illness for much of this life. So be it. I could do without the discomfort though. I look marvelous (said with Billy Crystal voice), so that's something at least.

I spoke of having a copy of *I Am That*, by Nisargadatta. Peter replies: "Have you seen *Prior to Consciousness*? Very lovely. Cancer came to Nisargadatta too, as you know. A dear friend used to say that our lives are but a moment, an eye blink and they are gone. I think she was right."

"Let's meditate together," I suggested to Peter. He said, "Perhaps let Alex be with us as well. Gentle Alex fills the sky with quiet. Her touch is with you always, and her eternal delight as she rolls in the grass is yours as well. How could it be otherwise?

She is the true presence in us all, manifested in cat form but unmanifested in eternal perfection.

She also likes to eat grasshoppers."

Always, Peter

# This, Too, Shall Pass

Wednesday was a nightmare. I got a new dental crown, which meant that I couldn't go to the doctor with Bob. Turns out that his disease is gaining the upper hand again, unless there has been a mistake in the lab. Tomorrow they will repeat the test, in hopes that it was wrong. In the meantime, his doctor will confer with someone about what to do next—if the chemo has quit working. To tell the truth, I am quite wiped out. I have run the emotional gamut and come up empty. I cried, talked too much and finally fell into bed exhausted.

Peter writes: "It seems you were asking how I have been doing. That's lovely of you. Sorry not to write, but I have been keeping pretty quiet with everyone. I have thought of you, though, and wondered how you and Bob are doing. I really hope Bob is better, and am keeping my fingers crossed for you both."

Ah, Peter, I hate to write and let you know. I have been trying to come out of a serious period of fear and discouragement since his last chemo failed. There are always lessons to learn and they are never easy when it involves life and death.

Bob received a high dose of chemo yesterday and is quite ill from it. We didn't sleep last night and as we sat together this morning, the thought came to me: *I do not need to know the future. I only need to know the now. An overturned glass, a sick dog, chemo nausea—sleep deprivation. This, too, shall pass.*

# Who Is the True Guru?

Peter and I sit by the fire of our mutual sufferings and warm ourselves as they burn brightly. He tosses in a log occasionally and so do I. The gist of it is that when you are being broken and there is no fixing you, what is left to do but be where you are? It is Peter who has been my guide to what is. He always says "Ho ho" after making a comment on his broken body. He never speaks about the details of his illness; only saying that he grows weaker and less able to write.

He knows me in a way that a person meeting me face-to-face never can. I tell him about losing my child, about going through chemo with my husband, and he understands. Last year when we had to put our dog, Christy, down, I asked Peter how old his cat, Alexandra, was. "She is younger than springtime," was his reply. Then he wrote, "Actually she is seventeen or eighteen, I forget."

We hit the send button on our little fireside chats, knowing that one day a silence will arise and Peter will have nothing left to say. In one sense, sorrow is the true guru, and when it burns away the dross of the self, only holy ash remains. I would like to think that someone would wander by our campfire and smear a bit on their forehead. Whether they do or don't will be of no concern to Peter. He would just say, "Ho ho."

## Peace Descends

Although I have spent years studying the great masters, it is always interesting to read the personal account of someone struggling to live the teachings. These books are not readily available because they are written by people who are unfamiliar with the publishing world. After I wrote *Life With A Hole In It*, it was rejected a couple of times because I was unknown. So after much trepidation, I decided to self-publish. I will be lucky to break even, but if I wanted to get the book out there, it was the obvious choice.

Why am I telling you this now? Because it is easy to be swamped with self-doubt about anything. During the years I was caring for my husband, the teachings seemed unfruitful to me. I was unable to follow them; rather, I was taken over by my personal anguish and all that it entailed. I felt myself to be a failure at the path and at the daunting job of being a caregiver.

Looking back, I see that I was being forged in the furnace of affliction and that I had no choice in the matter. Bob seemed to bear up under it better than I did. But even he did not make a full surrender, fighting his death right up until the end. He did not even have morphine except for a few days when he had no idea that he was being given it. A nosebleed was the only sign he had that he might be losing the battle. But inside there was massive bleeding.

I could not bear to be with him when he died;

he knew that. And I was spared by the mercy of my sister arriving just in time to sit with him the last day of his life. I was at home in a state of shock and exhaustion. I managed to make it through the funeral, the ice storm that followed and Christmas Day as a new widow.

I am still here learning my lessons. They are never-ending. But peace has descended amidst my struggles. It bids me rest and I often forget and get anxious and afraid again. And then I rest again. I am doing okay.

# Grace

Peter says that there is nothing that you can do to obtain grace. It either happens or it doesn't. That, too, is believable coming from his lips. It is as if he is saying, "Relax."

In a way, Peter is unfathomable. Perhaps you can feel his energy, too. It is an energy that twinkles as he speaks of a beloved cat with whom he hangs out. It is also an energy that simply tells the truth—about living with pain, about sitting in the sun, about being one with *what is*.

*Peter:* At satsangs most folks seemed to me to be describing a sort of new age or Buddhist version of heaven—none of which seemed like my cup of tea. Who on earth would wish for perpetual bliss—yuck, what a prison! I don't know—it just seems so much nicer (and a whole lot easier) to sit with a gentle cat friend.

If she is not chasing "enlightenment" then surely it is not worth chasing. She seems to like sleeping in the sun more than anything—at last, a philosophical school that makes some sense! Truly, it seems to me that we look so hard for a solution that we leave no room for one to enter.

## Remembering Myself

My calling is writing and also holding the still point as an energy practice. So I live a quiet life in order to be able to do that. And I am not noisy by nature, so it all works out. It's not that I dislike people; I dislike socializing for any extended period of time. I would not be the person with whom to spend a weekend. I run out of words and meaning. I am happier when I get home to my inner work. And a calling cannot be denied without paying a price. When Bob was sick during that long five-year period, sometimes I would say to him, "I know I am being called. I am just not sure what I am supposed to do." Of course I was called to just *be*. And that is how it goes.

But he was outgoing and, as the hospital chaplain told me, "He gets energy from people." So my life got considerably quieter after he died. And I was so exhausted that I took a couple of years to just learn how to sleep again.

Now each day offers itself up to me and I write or walk or putter around the house. I am always in touch with spirit, always watching my ego at work. It never gives up. It wants me to do things I don't want to do, like give a party or take a trip. Others do these things easily. Not me. But somehow it all works out. I write another essay, meditate for a while and get myself out the door for a walk. The spiritual path needs walkers, never mind how fast or slow they go. The pathless land can hold us all. If we remember ourselves, as Mr. Gurdjieff said, "Life is real." If not, it is a sham and that's a shame.

# A Grateful Amen

It is important for all outer teachings to fall away. This cannot happen until it happens. Before that, there is effort, struggle and being thrown off-balance. I experienced that with Vernon Howard, a master teacher if there ever was one. To meet him was to meet your own inner darkness up close and personal.

Oh, the frustration of setting out upon the true way. Oh, the dilemma of the civil war within. The skirmishes, the woundings and the battlefield stories told around the campfire. The enemy is everywhere but within. For what the teacher says is quickly forgotten as the battle rages. He did say that the foes are those of one's own household, but the outer ones are so much more easily seen.

But the true student perseveres. He keeps on keeping on though the battle rages. As Vernon said, darkness is always attacking light. The brighter the light, the greater the darkness. But the light shines on.

He has been gone for twenty years and what he taught is nothing less than Self-realization. He did not use that term; he shied away from any spiritual buzz words. Instead he taught his students how much ego hated the light of awareness, and how it would spend its last emotional dime to wage the war against what could save it.

Now I sit here at the keyboard knowing that the outer teachings arrive in any form they must and vanish when you least expect them to do so. What are you left with? A wordless experience, a shining forth, a blazing peace, a silent nod. A grateful amen.

# Hard Times

I wrote jokes for Joan Rivers as my young daughter went through three years of surgery, chemo and radiation. She died. I continued to write. I wrote a book called, *Laurie, One of the Lucky Ones*. She died. I changed the title to *Laurie, A Mother's Story*. I met a grief counselor who suggested that I write letters to her. That became *Letters to Laurie*. Fortunately I no longer have copies of those beginning books.

Now I was not only writing comedy, I was walking the spiritual path. I had a teacher who breathed fire at his students. That didn't bother me a great deal; it was nothing compared to the death of a child. I was learning to walk through the Children's Department at Macy's and not flinch too much as I saw the color pink. I threw myself into awakening like there was no tomorrow. I didn't change much.

Those first years without Laurie were hard ones indeed. I had to deal with my son's unexpressed grief, my husband's workaholic solution to mourning and my own increasing isolation from society. A saving grace for me was a Bichon Frise puppy that we got five weeks after our daughter died.

We moved across town to a new house. That house is now 34 years old. The dog got hit by a car and we got a new puppy. She lived to be over 16. We had to have her put to sleep while Bob was dying of his cancer. During these years I put one foot in front of the other – that was how I coped. I left my teacher's group when Bob was diagnosed. It was just too far to travel. My life was one big windshield and I was a tiny bug. Life being fair was out of the question. It was not even stormy. It was a tsunami in which I built a life raft out of the teachings and began writing essays as the waves pounded at it with fury.

Then the great silence began. It is not always pleasant but it is genuine. I have won my freedom. Did it the hard way. Hung in there. Kept the faith. Learned to know myself. Learned to know that simplicity and grace are the same thing.

I almost took a vacation and then realized that I am now on vacation every day. The waters are still. I have published two books. I am now what I would call a "real" writer. I know when to begin and when to end. Essays, that is. I have a GPS that shows me how to get to the blank screen and let my fingers do the talking. I hope that some of you are listening.

# The Great Silence

The great silence has happened gradually for me. I can't say much about it because it is, after all—silence! At first it is the silence of the tomb. I have been through that twice. The death of a child is a great silence, as is the death of a mate.

The ego fights mightily against the silence that could deliver it into wholeness. It is a great friction and a great fiction, the old ego, the old man or woman. Just look around at what you see in the media. The paparazzi are but one example. Everyone has a spin on things.

But the silence of death leads to the silence of the Self. "Die before you die," say the Sufis. The only way to this silence is through the constant practice of being the witness to all that the ego does.

Writing opens up the silence for a great many people who read my essays. I don't know how this works, but I just let the words flow until they stop. Very often someone will comment and say they felt a great relief after reading the essay. And I know that I was just a catcher for the words, a conduit for their own silence.

# Ho Ho!

Peter is undergoing his own torment; his doctors suspect that he is having many small seizures every day. Yet he encourages me by talking of watching the wind in the trees and feeling it on his skin. I love him like a brother and we only know each other through the internet. I lean my face against the monitor as if to gather some of his wry wisdom. We shall both go on, filing reports from the front, embedded reporters in the war against pain. If our reports make people uncomfortable, perhaps they are in need of a good cry themselves. There is no going to commercial in such a report, however. Someone has paid the price for all of this and one day we will be free. Until then, we talk and write and witness.

"I feel that little Alex does not know about duality or non-duality. Perhaps she finds such distinctions, umm, a tad unproductive? She does like to lie in the tall grass and play with insects, though. That makes real sense to her. The rest is just words, which in my experience she appears to care very little about. Ho ho!"

# The Blessedness of Letting Go

I was listening to Peter, Paul and Mary singing "Weave Me the Sunshine." It is one of my favorite songs and I think I know why. It is alluding to the highest kind of love of which the human heart is capable. Love that goes beyond the personal and reverberates throughout the cosmos. It is the "I am" set to music.

You know how it is—you love a friend or partner and yet they aggravate you. Your love isn't universal but particular. That is how we humans are wired. But once you lose a loved one, you are introduced to a wider and deeper kind of love, if you are lucky. When my husband died, at first I could only be glad that the suffering was over. I was kept busy dealing with the paperwork and chores connected with giving clothes away, reordering my life and all of that. I grieved but not totally, for in the beginning I sheltered myself against the storm of tears. I did this by remembering how he had aggravated me, how he had not lived up to his end of the bargain. I was going through all the stages of grief.

Now it is a few years later. I love him with a universal love. I have transcended the pettiness of the normal human marriage and now belong to love itself, as does he. When I write I also feel this deep love that is not possible between people in a personal relationship. My writing reaches beyond the borders of time and space and I am grateful for that. In that way we enter the mystery of universal connectedness without egos getting in the way.

## No One Ever Goes Away

Being a spiritual writer has its ups and downs. I live in both the spirit and the world, as do we all. Sometimes the world is dominant and vice versa. The trick is to ride out the storms without totally believing in them. Easier said than done. "It's time to stop treatment," is a hard storm. So is sleeping alone. But I am not alone in the higher sense.

The blank slate of awareness is fleshed out with the ego's business and shenanigans. The slate is forgotten time after time as we read what the ego writes on the slate. "More pie. Less budget. Gimme, gimme, gimme. I'm scared. Nobody loves me. I need a haircut. Pass the potatoes." That is where we live, after all.

I used to plug and unplug Bob's IV when he was in the chemo room and had to get up and move around. I fixed him dinner when we got back home. I used to think "What will I do after he is gone?" Now I know what I will do. I will breathe and write on the slate. It is only when I wipe it clean that everything makes sense. Love is not a four-letter word. It is a sense of eternity filtered through time and space. It occupies the heavens and the tiniest corner of a human heart. *I love you*, my spirit says to Bob, and he answers in a multitude of ways. He looks at me from a photograph and touches my tears when they run down my face. He moves through my heart enlivening these words. No one ever goes away.

# God Has a Sense of Humor

*"Laughter is carbonated holiness."*

Anne Lamott

*Peter:* Just getting over a week of cluster migraines—a happy legacy of some seizures a few years ago. When they come I am so hypersensitive that I must wear dark glasses and ear plugs and pretty much lie down and try not to breathe too loudly. Ho ho. A good time is had by all.

*Vicki:* I had a scare this week. Had to get a breast lump biopsied but it proved to be benign. Of course we were beside ourselves. Even suffering becomes old news, does it not?

*Peter:* Yes, God certainly has an interesting sense of humor. She is just a bundle of laughs sometimes. I suspect She may have been a Las Vegas comedienne at one time. I am so pleased that the lump was benign. Ah, living on the edge... who can say what will come and what will not? At this end things are difficult. Such is suchness.…

Alexandra loves to go and watch the water bubble by a little stream here. She and her brother Maple snuggle up together and watch the waters gurgle and froth. Most days after a hectic schedule of running and jumping between the stars, God stops by to sit with them... just soaking up the quiet peace of their presence. There by the stream, God and Alexandra and Maple. Love and nothing else.

It is either this or suffer. The only solace I have ever found is there by the stream, or rather, said another way—here, before creation starts up. Not in this moment—which seems a silly catch word—but rather before this moment. Before anything. Just sitting by the stream and watching the toss and tumble of it all. Just an easy, natural quiet. In this, all the rest—everything else—seems just various flavors of hell. Ha! This body flops and falls sometimes and gives Alexandra a start as she runs off amongst the tall grasses to hug the wind. So I follow her example, and forget everything for the joy of running (or in my case, crawling, ho ho).

Memory (whether of the past or of the future) is the presence of pain, is it not? But before memory happens, a spontaneous creation and quiet. Joy? Maybe. But that seems too complicated a term... just a lovely quiet. Oh heck, I don't know... sounds so silly in words... it just seems to me that there is something wonderful and so sweet... a sweetness that makes the suffering become less interesting after a while. Even whilst the body and silly mind may be yelling in pain.

I used to do stuff dealing with abstract mathematics. Now I cannot even count change in a store. If I hold to this loss, there is certainly suffering. But I do not need to count change when sitting with God and Alex and Maple by the stream, so what the heck. And since the stream is of course *Everything*, what the heck....

# A Wide Wildness

*Peter:* It is my own experience that most of the white-robed crowd, whether sanctimoniously trying to impress others in chat rooms online, or gathering in hushed wonder before the graven image of some beatific with big hair, have seen compassion or love from a great distance only. The blind cannot lead the blind. Associating with the mad seldom leads to sanity. They talk a great line, though, ho ho. And sound convincing. But there is a resonance between one heart and another that spins and dances only in the presence of the absence of two, or more precisely, of a "me." Ha! Like a small child in love with the sky, who knows she can fly. Like this—no logic is needed in the presence of life.

*Vicki:* I have been writing to a woman who used to be with Satchitananda and left very disillusioned.

*Peter:* In one's own heart (just my opinion of course), God is patiently waiting to jump out and say "Boo!" But for many the show seems so much more interesting. Especially when that show contains apparent love and suffering. We cry when the movie is intense and forget to eat popcorn or throw tomatoes at the screen.

*Vicki:* This woman appreciates what I have to say about the path in general and how isolating it turns out to be in the final analysis.

*Peter:* It seems to me that we follow a path until we make our own. A lion makes its own path, an ant meekly follows the path of another ant. What a giggle it all is.

*Vicki:* I told her that you have found the sweetness in life, whereas we have not. Now I ask you, Peter, is that fair!

*Peter:* Well, well, it seems to me that we would all benefit greatly if we kissed more cats, or at least a llama or emu or hawk or rabbit or parrot or dog or any true innocent. I ask you, how can anyone not fall in love with those little faces? Ah, but we hold back from love, don't we? And since love is what we are (yes!)—not in a silly intellectual way, but in actual fact—love here meaning ease and laughter and a quiet lightness—falling in love every time one can is such an easy tumble into oneself. I don't know... we suffer and we laugh and we cry and we live. It all flows and it all goes.

In the absence of a presence of a 'me' there is a wide wildness bigger than the sky. The brain is such a waste of space. The heart leaps and runs and hugs so freely. It takes the brain by the hand and leads it into wonder. Ho ho!

# A Quiet Vibrancy

Hi Vicki,

It seems you were asking how I have been doing. That's lovely of you. Sorry not to write—but I have been keeping pretty quiet with everyone. I have thought of you, though, and wondered how you and Bob are doing. I really hope Bob is better, and am keeping my fingers crossed for you both.

There is little new at this end: The latest iatrogenic pontifications suggest I may be having dozens of small seizures a day. However, since I can no longer afford their expensive treatments, they are unable to say for sure. Ho ho, as if effect could ever have a cause. What silliness.

The sky still sparkles and the cats still dance through the grasses. Deer come and nuzzle the roses. In everything there is a quiet vibrancy. I watch the birds in the trees—lovers at the kiss of the sky. What else is there?

# Consolation from Peter

I told Peter that we had to have our beloved dog, Christy, put down. Before Rob and I drove her to the vet, Rob insisted that she be fed a few bites of chicken, one of her favorite treats. His Japanese friend said, "I alway remember her putting her paws on the chair, as if to say 'Give me chicken!'" Here is Peter's reply:

*Peter:* How blessed you are to have been so loved, and to be able to so love. The cats here prefer fish to chicken, but they would not turn either down. They appear to be particularly fond of food that can still walk a little. Compassion is all very well, but they seem to feel that food is food whether in a tin or still trying to escape. All I can say is that I am eternally grateful that this body is bigger than theirs.

*Vicki:* I feel my powerlessness, yet I know that I am still trapped in the "me."

*Peter:* Perhaps what you are is what Christy saw in you, rather than what you believe. It is my experience that some folks equate awakening (whatever that word means—maybe an imagined escape from pain) with the freedom to be what they believe an awakened person to be. Did I say that right?

I feel that the whole concept of awakening may be a kind of strange nightmare. It is astonishing that one person could be considered enlightened or awake and another, not. Sort of like saying Sandra (the oldest cat here) is trapped in her "me" and Christy was not. Just doesn't seem to make any sense. Perhaps we like the idea of the mind understanding, and so forsake the heart, which has no need of understanding anything.

When I was younger, getting food was not always easy. I remember being a tad hungry once and watching some raccoons around three in the morning walking across some roofs. Very lovely. They never knew from one day to the next if they would be eating or starving, but they were so alive and splendid, framed by the moonlight.

Hmmm—I've forgotten if there was a point to this little story. Maybe just the wonder of how their beauty absolutely drowned out my own hunger? Sorry, not much of a point, but it's all that seems to be popping up.

Well, I am girding my loins to help load the car with garbage for the monthly trip to the dump. There is no garbage pickup here, so at the beginning of each month, we load everything that cannot be recycled and drive 31 miles out to the nearest dump site. An enjoyable experience that no one should miss—the smell at the dump alone is worth the trip.

I hope Bob is doing well. And you, too.

Always, Peter

## Temporary Good News

Dear Peter, After this message got bounced twice, I sent it to you at your website address.

Peter: Oops, sorry. Between doctors, getting ready to move and inability to afford my email account anymore, things sort of got away.

Vicki: You weren't going to leave me high and dry, I hope.

Peter: Really now, how could that ever happen? Unless of course a cat falls on my head and kills what's left.

Vicki: Haven't heard from you this week.

Peter: Just weak. It takes me a long time to do things lately. I think that if reincarnation works, then I may return as a very slow-moving rock. It seems to me that rocks appear generally to be a rather peaceful race, loving the warmth of the sun and the dance of the clouds overhead. It has been my experience too that the average rock is more observant, loving and open to life than many, but I may well be mistaken.

*[I recounted a story of how I got lost in the hospital parking lot... I started down the steps and couldn't quite figure out where I was."]*

Peter: I loved your story of your parking garage adventure! It sounds like when you sat down and stopped looking, the car just came to you; but that's probably a complete misrepresentation of events.

Vicki: The good news is that Bob's blood work was okay.

Peter: This is wonderful news!

Vicki: The bad news is that he can't wash the dishes.

Peter: Ah yes. And yet somehow I cannot quite imagine how getting out of washing the dishes may be entirely a bad thing.

Vicki: We are still sad about Christy, which is to be expected.

Peter: I am so sorry for this. It can be difficult to lose a loved one, especially one who loves back so freely. I would guess that she lived her life without the knowledge that one day she would die, and so escaped much effort.

Vicki: I am ready for a brief patch of sunlight before heading into the next tunnel....

Peter: There is a lovely story which you may have heard of a guru who was asked about the proper way to pray. He answered that one correct prayer was worth a lifetime of incorrect prayer.

"Ah, but how does one pray correctly?" he was

asked. "By sitting in the sun and falling asleep," was his answer. I love this. I always knew cats knew how to prey!  Always, Peter

# Ease

Peter: It is my little experience that what appears to occur simply does so, whether we fight it, embrace it, or vomit purple stuff all over it, ho ho. After appearance appears, it is gone. No cause, no effect. No relation of one thing to another. It seems to me that no special thoughts encourage grace, no special grace encourages thoughts. What a giggle! Striving, and perhaps more especially, spiritual striving, it seems to me, is the association of past and future as if they were connected—and all at the expense of hearing the laughing lilt of the wind as it nuzzles Alexandra's fur and sneezes.

That which can be gained can also be lost. Speaking personally—and this is just my opinion of course—only that which is permanent is of interest. God dies when I fall asleep at night, so She is of no interest. Teachers die too, as do their teachings, so they are of no interest. Insights also fade, so they are of no interest. The story of one's life, love, hate, religious fervor, knowledge, self… all fade, so they are blind avenues too. The fun question it seems to me is what lasts—what is permanent? Anything other than that, (just my opinion), is not really as tasty as pie… oops, I meant to say "the sky", which is also pretty sweet.

It seems to me that truth (perhaps with a capital T) is so simple and easy that we run past it, sweating heavily. The love of a little cat in one's arms as you snooze together on the sunlit grass is, I feel, more profound and lasting, than all the world's holy books and thousand year old teachings. Ho ho.

To me—just my opinion again—ease is simple, obvious, permanent, and always present. The tortures of one's apparent life, sated and abated. So simple, just to relax with a little cat and breathe the sunlit days as they appear to pass. Tomorrow, if it comes, will take care of itself.

Peter

# Downhill Fast

We were heading downhill fast. The cancer had picked up speed in Bob's bone marrow. He was living only by the grace of packed platelet transfusions. Me, I was living only by a frayed string of effort.

We are sitting in the great room.

"Can't you cry?" I said, desperately. "We're being parted!"

Bob had been unable to cry for the longest time. But I needed to see his tears; otherwise, it would just be me lost in this coming deluge.

He looked at me, every muscle in his body limp, spent. And tears formed in his eyes and finally made it down to his cheeks.

My own crying tasted salty and futile. There was nothing left but fatigue and honesty.

# The Show Must Go On

*This is our human predicament and the only consolation is embracing it.*

Leonard Cohen

Bob was now being kept alive by transfusions. We were worn to a nub. The week before Christmas of 2004, he was admitted to hospice and died four days later. He did not go gently into that good night. He climbed out of bed trying to "get up to the second floor" and there was none. I am told he fought vigorously in the last hours of his life, but I had gone home, unable to face them.

Exhaustion demanded my absence from the scene and I feel that destiny played a hand in that as well. My sister from Pennsylvania appeared right on schedule to insist that I go home and rest.

My friend, Aile Shebar, saw the photo of Bob I posted online after he was quite ill. In her words:

"Because I have nothing to compare his likeness to in the past I can tell you what I see, through the subtle tearing of my eyes, now. He is noble—looking directly into the eyes of the photographer, and they speak volumes of space, of the vastness we come and go from, and an openness.

There is a hint of a smile, and the innocence of a child. Rather than the hands you miss, which were large and strong, he has the sculpted hands an artist and they are beautiful in fact. I see a kindness and a willingness, in that moment of the picture taking, to be present. And that is how I feel him today, present—present through this thread, present in your heart, and present in all of ours as well. We are touched by your love and your words, Vicki."

# A Diamond Tear

I talk to Bob at night before I go to bed. I ask him for help and say I love him. This makes me feel connected to what is eternal. I also bless myself as if I were another person altogether. Then I end another simple day. Writing and launching my books, I am more hopeful than I have been in a long time. I feel they will develop wings and go on a journey that I will enjoy.

Bob came to me in a dream recently and let me know that I was doing fine, spiritually speaking. He wanted me to be less passive toward life and so I am going to share my message freely from this point on with whoever wants it. It is so simple. Everything is in the hands of God.

Everything given to God is returned to us on a higher plane. When I am reunited with my lost loves, we will not recognize each other for our beauty.

It is only some years later that his tenderness blesses me unexpectedly. How can that be? He's dead, after all. The quality of the soul is eternal; it is able to reach down into hearts on earth that feel quite alone. And his soul is tending mine like you wouldn't believe. It reminds me that he never was anything but supportive of my writing, that he asked me to find my passion before he died (and writing was that passion). His presence surrounds me with this house that he paid for and the son we raised together. And when I cry a diamond tear, it is often because of his undying love.

For you readers who follow my essays, I express my tenderness in these little notes written without a certain someone coming in to look over my shoulder. But then again, who knows? I would like to think that, when I married a six-foot-four-inch Georgia Tech man who thought a slide rule was interesting, I knew what I was doing. I didn't, for no one ever knows what deals are being struck. I used to think if I had known he would die such a terrible death, I wouldn't have married him. But in reality there is no such luxury of choice. And since I am on the path of awakening, I now know that love lies far above the realm of choice.

Saying "I do" is not something a person in their twenties does consciously. When Bob came to me after his death in a dream and said to me, "Your prayers are written on the wall of my heart every day," I realized what our marriage had been about. It was about coming to terms with what love really is. It is something we are, and in the last analysis, is better off undefiled by the ego's touch.

His glasses are now in a box of mementos that I have saved. But the eye that looked on me with love is the one that sees the sparrow, too, with love. Tenderness: who doesn't need some? It comes in small things, not large. It lingers in the heart, expanding it to infinity. It says "I love you" in ways that defy logic. And that's a good thing.

# Dreams of Love

It's winter and I'm sitting in my cozy chair with the footstool and saying to myself: *I own this house.* I look up to the four long clerestory windows that let in the sunlight. I feel sad and try to figure out why, in this particular moment, sorrow has come wafting back into me once again.

Suddenly these thoughts materialize: *Did he feel a sadness as he was leaving the house in the ambulance that would take him to hospice? Did he realize it was the last time he would be there?* I felt the sorrow shroud me. We never had a real conversation about what his death would be like. He didn't say many of the things I wish he had. There was nothing like the lines you hear in the movies. Instead he was silent, his strength waning, his words lying as dormant as his body was becoming.

Grief can never be fully put into words. Because love is not about the words. It's about the music. There is a dirge in my heart as I allow myself to remember the devastation that I felt and still feel at times. We were deeply in love and yet we put distances between us to minimize the sorrow. I know that. We each built walls to keep the other's wall from toppling over. I know he would have liked to reach out to me more than he did. Soon I would be living without him. His clothes would no longer hang in the closet and I would quickly fill up the space they used to take. That is a woman's dream—to have enough closet space. I kept his bathrobe for a while and would put my face against it and would end up using it to wipe my tears away.

Don't let anyone tell you that you should get over your sorrow. Yes, it waxes and wanes, but the love inside is never deleted and thrown in the trash. I am getting older without him. There will be no more back rubs on a cold winter's night or his pills to put in the little box or a certain look on his face that said it all: I am leaving you now; I will always love you. And then I had a dream visitation where he said, "Your prayers are written on the wall of my heart every day." Amen.

## Dwindling Down to Nothing

The physical body eventually dwindles down to nothing Some end up in God's Waiting Room, Florida. Others move around in airstream trailers or on luxury liners bound for "exotic" ports. Plaid shorts, dark socks and funny caps are the men's uniform, while their female counterparts go for winter wear of sweatshirts with cardinals on them and Chico outfits in the summer. Dull City, dwindling down to nothing.

I find myself looking at the skin on my arms and thinking: I wish I could get that removed. "That" being the latest little patch of brown or white, the reminder that I am just passing through. Even online, while death of the ego is an ongoing conversation, ironically discussion about the death of the body is avoided. Ageism is the last "ism" to face.

We prefer our gurus young or dead; we definitely don't want them covered in liver spots. Even J. Krishnamurti had a troop of women who anointed his hair with almond oil and kept him impeccable. U.G. Krishnamurti died looking ancient, emaciated and frail. My teacher, felled by cancer, became childlike and would sneak into the office just to hang out with his students. Life is not a barrelful of laughs or wisdom. It is more like a creaky machine running slower and slower. That old song, "The Merry-Go-Round Broke Down", comes to mind.

I am sure if Jesus had lived long enough, someone would have had to prompt Him on the Beatitudes.

"Blessed are the… what?" Buddha would have had to wear a Medic Alert bracelet and Krishna would have scooted around in a walker with a basket.

Now I am laughing instead of crying. The only therapy there is for growing old.

# A Jeweled Net of Grace

Today I am remembering how badly I failed Bob when he was ill and dying. I cannot minimize this; I was really angry and exhausted for years. The grief ran like blood through the streets of my heart. I forged ahead knowing that death would eventually outrun him. Who wouldn't be angry?

I am now beginning my ninth year of life without him. How have I changed? It is hard for me to see or know. My friend, Tallulah, says that she has watched a great change happen in me. She sees how I have become more than a wife or more than a caregiver. I often feel stuck and powerless. I walk on.

My life is my own now. I run it well. But at night bad dreams still arise. They are usually shame-based. A childhood shame rooted in trying to please my mother, apparently. She is dead; the shame is alive in the unconscious. I circle myself with white light.

My Mac is where I find answers arising. Of course, it serves as a bridge between my heart and mind. My fingers find themselves walking peacefully and quickly over the keys. I want to share with the reader. I want to connect with them softly and in a healing way. To do this I must become vulnerable and open.

It is sad that I feel I must be a good soldier rather than one who gracefully surrenders to what is. I am still mounting a defense against my ultimate surrender. It might involve an even deeper suffering, a cleansing of everything I am clinging to.

I have been given proof that I am not alone. That I can live peacefully and meaningfully. Yet the child within does not quite believe that. She draws back from being seen and heard. She hides behind the veil of the mind while her heart is standing there in plain sight. I am a mind-fish caught in a jeweled net of grace.

# Self-Kindness

*Peter writes:* I feel that the so-called 'holy' people, those who think they are teachers—you know, flowing robes on a comfy satsang couch—when speaking of ways to handle illness or misfortune are for the most part talking through their hats.

I have heard them talk of grief and how to handle it: perhaps let it flow through, perhaps go into it, or perhaps ignore it. Ah yes—that famous psychological expertise! I have heard talk of physical pain, too, and how to handle it: perhaps let it flow through, perhaps go into it, or perhaps ignore it. To my ears, it's all talk.

They do not know—no one does. Each individual, I feel, is different in how they approach difficulties. For myself, none of what they say makes sense. What does make sense to me is light in the trees, a cat's purr, and the obviousness of the gentleness behind everything, even the apparent misfortunes. I have been literally screaming in pain in the hospital after surgery which went wrong. And yet, and yet, behind it all such a stillness and a joy. Sigh. Sounds crazy I'm sure.

*Vicki:* My attitude is fearful and I cannot change that on my own. Lord knows I would like to. I am a sissy.

*Peter:* In this we are all children. My only suggestion, for what it's worth, is to take what comfort you can find wherever and in whomever you can find it. It is my experience that few people are kind to themselves. I would gently suggest that perhaps the greatest good you can do, is be kind and loving to yourself.

## Going With the Flow

So how do I move beyond grief? If I try, I will be using mental effort, which is not a power. I move beyond it by being it in the moment. I go with it, loving myself for re-experiencing the loss of someone significant in my life. Gone forever, not coming back, not here to fix things, to comfort me. I am not cast down but lifted up by love.

Love is holding me like a jewel in the palm of its hand. It is regarding me with infinite grace, encouraging me to bloom into my full soul beauty. It has been a rough and harrowing road, but there are also moments of sublimity. When I sit and write easily of both love and death. When I know that my path is unique to me and unfolding exactly as it should. If you are grieving or fearing loss, there is not a thought in the world that will heal you. That is the lesson in grief. Thought is for practical things; for the spirit, awareness is needed.

I move around my house; it's the same house that fitted around our lives so nicely and yet it's an empty house—empty of a husband. I fit it snugly these days. Its cedar sides are full of bird holes and I fear the arrival of the Pileated Woodpecker that can do damage in minutes. I would not be so aware of the house if I still had a husband to be "in charge." That was his job; the outside of the house, the car and yard maintenance. I was the cook and shopper, the bill payer. And we lived side by side in the mystery.

We balanced each other and now I must balance myself. My masculine side is called in when boards are damaged, when the car needs air in the tires. I am learning to live more practically. But because I am alone, I am more in tune with what God would have me do. I write more because I have more time. I share myself with readers in an intimate way. I am not here to teach anyone anything. I am here because the river flows and I am going with it, not against it. What does love have to teach but letting go and entering the stream?

## Only Peace Lies Ahead

Essentially we are transmitting love all day long, for that is what we are receiving from our higher selves. We try to block it out with thoughts that revolve around our powerlessness, our "not-good-enough-ness." But once we surrender to the inevitability and eternality of love, we are in for a shower of blessings. That sounds trite; but who doesn't want them?

Bob and I were in lock step for many years. His cancer diagnosis began to break the cadence. He became slow and I became faster, faster. I ran harder and harder to fill the demands that being a caregiver entails. I became angry and exhausted and, finally, sorrowful. I clutched at what used to be and found nothing but emptiness. So after he died, I became the emptiness. I spent several years taking care of business and the new norm. I lived simply and quietly, always hoping that God would show me the way to share myself with others.

Now I know that I am to do small things, not big. Careful things, not expansive ones. Inner things, not outer ones. I am learning to be myself in the midst of inner chaos. There is still a chasm to leap. And one day it will be time. I am not even sure what it is, what it is made of. I go to my Tai Chi class and out for an occasional lunch with friends.

In the meantime I write about my inner life and what it is feeling like on any given day. I am trying to share the marrow of myself. Bob's cancer was of the bone marrow; odd as that is, it is a fact. In his bones he was dying and now in my bones I am living as God would have me live. Sharing the spirit of dry bones come to life. Singing the notes of *hallelujah* and *amen*. I like to think that I have survived the worst times of my life; that only peace lies ahead.

## You Are What Bob Is

I had been hearing from Peter less and less often; he, too, was weakening as the days went by. By now we knew what we meant to each other. As he had told me in the very beginning of our friendship, "For what it's worth, I hold your hand in this."

When I let Peter know of Bob's death, this was his reply:

He is missed. It seems to me that what remains, of course, is love. His love for you and yours for him. That always lasts. Life must have loved him dearly to take him into itself.

It seems that we are in a rowboat without oars, adrift on the river. What can we do? The current carries us, sometimes through smooth water, sometimes through rough. But it is all out of our control, no matter what we do, what we think, what we understand. So we go, carried we know not where, carried we know not how. Adrift under the clear bright stars, awed by the wide wild sky as we look up and see the stars shimmer and dance in their glory.

You are what Bob is.

Love, Peter

# Keeping Busy

Peter was growing weaker.

*Vicki:* I miss hearing from you but understand completely.

*Peter:* Hi dear Vicki,
   Yes, I continue to be ill, hence writing is pretty much a challenge. Life may not always appear to be the bundle of smiles and giggles that was originally advertised. Perhaps a consumer protection agency should be established.

*Vicki:* I can't let go of suffering until I am able, can I?

*Peter:* Well, I kinda feel that suffering is on the whole simply a path of more suffering. I cannot see how suffering leads anywhere else. Toni, who likes to have people call her by the name of a river in India, told me once that she had never experienced real physical pain. Yet she keeps telling people to dive more deeply into the pain anyway. Hmmm, perhaps the tea should be sipped before declaring it tasty.
   Ho ho. I see no point to suffering. It seems such a drag. Someone said to me recently, as I was trying not to fall down again, that I must be really angry at life to be suffering so much. For a moment I thought she must be talking to someone else, but no; she apparently meant what she obviously mistook for

me. I started to giggle. Poor thing thought I must be cracking up.

Suffering? No thanks. Why would anyone want to do that? I sit with little Alexandra on the green green grass. We watch the dance of the butterflies together and sing. Sometimes I have breath and play my flute under an open sky. Even when things are a tad difficult, sunlight and song are always available, don't you feel? Just a small shift in attention from the antecedent to the causeless quiet. Oh, sure, I yell and carry on when needed. But suffering? No thank you.

# No Time or Space

There is a key here somewhere that I am trying to play. When Bob was alive, our love was just as human as anyone else's. There were good times and bad, roughs days and smooth. But overall, it was just garden variety love. Now he is gone and my love for him grows daily. What is the key to this mystery? There are no bodies involved. When the body fell away, the love remained. At first I was in shock and later I built a wall around my heart as I had done when our daughter died.

Now the wall is gone and the love has rushed to fill the space. What is the key but absence of ego? Absence of the body equals the full presence of eternity. It is an awesome void he left that is filled with presence. It isn't his or mine; that is also a key. It is a radiating out from center to center. There is no periphery, no time or space.

I sit here with a mug of coffee looking out at a cold December day. Bob and Vicki have parted. This body types what the spirit says is so. Who am I to argue with that?

I'm really writing for myself. My friend Monica, who is psychic, said the more I wrote, the faster I would heal. And I love to write; it is my therapy and my passion. Here I sit allowing words to emerge from innocent fingers who do not know the score. They are just serving the moment.

So Christmas is one week from today and I am

on edge. I have never liked holidays and the fact that Bob died on December 20, 2004, doesn't help. I have eaten too much fudge, felt too much sadness and am now exasperated because a chuck roast refuses to get tender. I put it in the crock pot early this morning and it is as tough as I would like to be.

I have eaten fudge and cookies and all kinds of sugary *no nos* that march straight to my stomach and stay there. There is nothing on TV but reruns and the usual Saturday fare. I am reading a good book but it is almost finished. Then what will I do?

Are you waiting for me to say for the hundredth time that I miss being married? I do. Although I am on the spiritual path, I had a mate who was, too. That is unusual. I am sure he doesn't want me to grieve but to enjoy my life. Enjoyment, for me, is a simple thing. It happens or it doesn't. Nothing complicated interests me. I write simply and quickly. I cook the same way. In fact, I am both simple and quick (insert a grin). I am also slow to move on, to try new things or shake things up. It's a wonder I have learned to balance my life in any way at all. Inwardly I may always walk alone, but I have learned to try and do it gracefully.

Now I love him with a universal love. I have transcended the pettiness of the normal human marriage and now belong to love itself, as does he. When I write I also feel this deep love that is not possible between people in a personal relationship. My writing reaches beyond the borders of time and space and I am grateful for that. In that way we enter the mystery of universal connectedness without egos getting in the way.

# A Gentle Simplicity

*Vicki:* I was out walking and talked to a neighbor who has a white cat that adopted her. The flowers were bright around the cat—a lovely scene. She was planting some flowers and the cat was just there being beautiful.

*Peter:* This is so lovely. This is what I see—just this gentle simplicity of love in everything. Habits and such may hang on. So what? I would much rather not be ill or poor. Or so incredibly handsome. Hmmm, wait a second—maybe I'll keep that last one, ho ho! And yet ill and debilitated or strong and active, I am always happy when God stops by, with cats and sunlight tugging at Her hair; so I look at this and laugh. We all fade, sooner or later. So be it.

My wife is off for a couple of days' vacation. I am so happy that she can get away for a bit. I promised her I would be here when she returns, so she left with a lighter heart. Little Maple (Alexandra's brother) has been so kindly caring for me by catching small baby rabbits and bringing them to my feet on the living room carpet. So loving is he to do this. Ha! Although it appears that rabbits have a different view of this. Ha! Viewpoints and opinions. Lots of fun to play with, but what a weight to place upon oneself if believed. God juggling rabbits and humans between Her tender hands. Who knows which will fall first? But She juggles with such obvious mirth, that one cannot help but smile whilst careening through the sky.

# An Awake Heart

*An awake heart is like a sky that pours light.*

Hafiz

Knowing that you are bigger than the sky is a gift that you share spontaneously. Peter never intended to become like this—it just happened. Effortlessly he knew that his being extended itself into infinity.

As a boy he was poor, standing in the cold parking lot of a library, waiting to get in so that he could use the washroom to keep himself clean. I can picture him soaking up knowledge as eagerly as he did the free water coming from the faucet. He always appreciated the little things.

I never knew him when he was small, but to know him now is to believe what he tells you. He speaks of the beauty of a raccoon running over the rooftops and his feeling of awe at such a sight. He talks about his cat named Alex who is the quintessence of love. We are with Peter as he sits in the sun feeling the wind on his skin. He conveys the simplicity of his life with a nod or a grin.

Peter never speaks of his prognosis, other than to say it is poor. I know it is worse than poor. His brilliant mind is hampered by the conditions of an impaired body. What he gives us all is a frank benef-icence born of courage and surrender. It takes a great deal of courage to let go when one has almost nothing left. That nothing is even more precious. To let go of it is a monumental decision. When he lets go, we feel his love. Ah, Peter, you are indeed bigger than the sky!

# The Nub of a Wing

My inner life is changing, reordering itself around a new core. Hard to put it into words because it is such a simple thing. I don't think as much as I used to. That leaves me empty much of the time, but in a good way.

I have apparently made a soul decision to stand firmly on the shores of my new life. A life where I am at the center and not my mind. This feels redeeming and fruitful and mysteriously destined. As you know, I have been putting myself through the wringer for many years. And now, well, I fancy that a nub of a wing is poking through the wringer. Could it be? Yes, it feels like real growth into the mystery. Into the elevation of the soul to its rightful place. Perhaps there are small crocus bulbs waiting to sprout at my feet.

I am no spring chicken but that just means my new growth is all the more precious. I see myself in a kinder light, as if I had taken out the glaring bulb of thought and put in a rose-colored lower wattage one. The lines erased from my brow and my shoulders a bit more relaxed. Oh, the mirror doesn't like me any better; it's just that my song is softer now.

I bought this bright blue coat that I love just because it isn't black. Fancy that. I went to T. J. Maxx and bought goodies like lebkuchen, lemon cookies and coconut ones. I have made cups of cinnamon tea and savored the flavor of this new life.

Now for the mystery part of the essay. Are you

ready, dear reader? I am inviting Bob to speak from the other side.

"Dear Angel, you are not about to believe we are apart. Never have we been apart since I fell truly, madly and deeply in love with you in fourth grade. So sweet you are, so young at heart. Your aura is the most beautiful song I have ever heard."

"I didn't know that auras made music."

"Oh, I see you as pure music. Pure grace and rhythm.

"You had a tin ear," I said.

"I was blocking out much of my sensitivity. I didn't learn that until I crossed over. Now I hear beautiful music every day and see colors without human names."

"I have to decide where to go on my next adventure," I said. "I am thinking about California."

"You are free now. You may go or stay. You may come or go. You may speak or be silent. Just know that this is your time now. Let no one convince you otherwise, especially the voices in your head that would condemn you."

And so, my love, my beloved Bob, now when I do my exercises at night, I no longer look at your side of the bed and feel tears welling up. Instead I look right at the middle of it, seeing us together in truth. And so it is and so it shall be. Amen

# The Other Side—A Meditation

*When a woman is awakened*
*she melts and perishes.*

Rumi

"You have mastered death twice, yet you have not walked upright onto the shore of the Sea of Sadness. Your husband and daughter are waiting for you, but you have always been too exhausted by your journey through the sorrow to meet them.

Your husband is showing me the symbol of a wheelchair. He is kicking it over the cliff so you can stand in your own strength and mastery. Your daughter is holding a small stuffed toy and a balloon."

"What about my son?" I asked the guide.

"He already sees this; he is merely waiting for you to see it, too. He looks to you, the mother and the matriarch, and sees your sadness. But now you have been given a new life, one where you are strong and reunited with your loved ones."

That was several nights ago. The meditation was guided by a gifted psychic. Although some of you may be skeptical, I am not. It has turned the key to a new doorway for me. For the past several nights I have been having fruitful dreams. I can only be grateful I took this inner journey.

You feel a softness in the energy of these words. I know that because I feel it as well.

I have crossed the sea of sadness and am now

standing on the shore of the other side. And I see now that separation is only in the mind. There IS no other side. It's all one.

# You Are the Self

*Vicki:* Things must go on just exactly as they do. I must fret and fear and get mad... until I don't anymore. This is my *sadhana*, you might say... to know my actual condition.

*Peter:* It seems to me—just my opinion, of course—that we do not have an actual condition. Just some thoughts that cascade in an apparent connection from past to predicted future. Thoughts cannot exist now—they are always before or after, don't you feel? Little Alexandra cat just came in for a chat, but when she saw me typing, she wandered off. Like this—a thought comes, natters on a bit, then wanders off. And we think we are that thought and hug it as if that poor dead thing can ever give us comfort or warmth. Ho ho. Little Alex is so much nicer to hug. And so much more real. Nisagardatta said once that people keep busy because they find it difficult to bear their own consciousness.

This seems right—we think and we think and we think we know and we think we don't know and we think some more, all in a quite wonderful effort to avoid joy. Which, it seems to me, is what we truly are. Not in a big hoo-ha, new-agey way, ho ho, but rather in the quiet joy of listening to a bubbling stream in the sunlight, with a cat or two teasing the nose with furry hugs.

Of course apparent tragedy happens. We lose loved ones and we mourn. Or we are born with a genetic predisposition to depression. Or we are seriously ill. Or a loved one is ill. Or whatever. And yet, and yet, it seems to me that the availability of respite is always present. And that respite, I feel, is more likely to be found by making one's own path.

I have a picture my wife took of some nearby mountains on my wall, and under it I have typed something Ramana Maharshi once said:

*You are the Self now and can never be anything else. Throw your worries to the wind, turn within and find peace.*

If we wait for grace, it may come. But now is so much more fun, don't you feel? A small shift in attention, from the pain to its Source. Ho ho!

It is hard to get any clearer than Peter was. Through the maelstrom of my suffering he spoke to me. He listened to me. He manifested wisdom. How does one repay a friend like that? Perhaps to bow quietly in deference to his magnanimous nature. The friend who sat in the yard and played a toy flute while cats slept on his chest. Not to mention his bravery in the face of what the doctors told him: "Your prognosis is grim."

Peter turned away from physicians in order to heal himself, with the help of his feline friends. He was not kidding when he said his little cat knew more about helping him than they did. He did not mince words on that score. At some point, one throws in the mental towel and plays in the field of Now.

That is the only place I can locate my friend Peter.

\* \* \* \* \*

It was so effortless to communicate with Peter. Our correspondence went on for several years. This I know: Every time I read his words I come more alive. Although he is gone, the attar of awareness permeates the pages. He was the simplest of writers and the strongest.

When one is suffering, an ally in awareness is invaluable. Someone who can cut through the ropes of reality to reveal the light creating everything. I just watched Nic Wallenda cross the Grand Canyon on a high wire. Peter danced across the wire of his illness with the same surety. Oh, he fell with regularity, but he was just in his front yard....

Sometimes people say they like the simplicity of my words. I had the complexity knocked out of me, thank God. Now the bare bones remain. But dry bones dance... now hear the words of the Lord, as the old hymn says.

Peter, dear Peter. In your absence you have become presence.

## The Illusion of Time

I woke up early this morning. Sliced a banana and ate it with a piece of coffee cake. As I sat at the table, I looked at the small travel alarm clock sitting there. It died, after a faithful run of probably thirty years. In a small black plastic case, it shows me that the time is now permanently 10:06. There are four hands on this little throwback of an analog clock. I tried putting new batteries in it, but they simply had no effect. Now, as I eat a meal, I can look over and see that it is still exactly 10:06. Proves that time, whether being accurately measured or not, is still an illusion!

It's on the kitchen table simply because that is where I put it to try out the new batteries. Peter came to know the eternal. His clock, so to speak, was always showing the same time. That is why you can read his words again and again and they remain ever-fresh. When I listen to the recording of him playing the toy flute, it is always now.

Who knows what would happen if we truly returned to our natural state? In the mornings I revel in the silence. The sun filters through the trees in a primeval way. My thoughts lie dormant as I allow my fingers to unfold the words like fronds. The words are mere shadows playing upon the screen.

Peter and I linked arms, held hands and saw each other in the most basic possible way. We could communicate the eternal truth without the need of measurement. He had seen that everything is an illusion, including our ideas about God and love. What was left over was the loaves and fishes of the living moment. It continues to feed us all.

# The Ultimate Luxury

Peter discovered the ultimate luxury—being himself. As he held my hand during Bob's illness, that is all he did. His words, as evidenced in this emails, were merely evidence that he was present. There is a house-cleaning that happens when ego goes. Even though Peter helped his wife take garbage to the dump, he had none of his own.

When I would tell him of my suffering, he would always accept it. By so doing, his validation helped removed it. Suppression is a worthless tool, after all. He knew suffering as being ever present. He just chose to let it move through him.

There is no way I cannot see the robins run on the grass. No way I cannot recognize the truth of my being. Some days I am able to grasp the connection between one life and another without the mind causing static. I rest in that deep knowing.

It is hard to be oneself because society imposes so many penalties against it. But Peter was suddenly jerked from society and therein lay his freedom. He had been a good student of the Way; now he became it.

So many nights I received comfort from this good man. I still do.

# The Core of the Heart

I keep trying to wrap up this book with one grand essay. Peter would say *ho ho* or maybe even *ho hum*. He was just not into grand displays. It was the quiet moments that bore the sweetest fruit for him.

So many of my days and nights were filled with terror while Bob was dying. Exhaustion was something I lived with. Burnout was my middle name. At one point before resuming chemo, Bob had to have his gall bladder removed. I curled up in the fetal position, crying into the phone. On the line was the oncology social worker. She was a great solace to me. "I just can't go," I wailed. So I didn't. And Bob fell down on a marble floor while walking into the Outpatient Surgery Unit. They had to stop and X-ray his knees before they would operate. As it was, the surgeon called me at midnight after the surgery saying, "We have to take him back in. He's bleeding everywhere we touched him. He is a very sick man." As if I didn't know that.

My friends thought I was losing it because I could not get dressed and be at the hospital like a dutiful wife. One invited me to come stay at her house, after she had been informed by another friend about my fragility. I was insulted. And the last thing I needed was to be around happy helpful people. I was drowning and that didn't feel like a rope.

So I would write Peter and he would talk about Alex and Maple and how he had fallen down again.

It was so gentle, so healing for me. Just to block out the dire prophecies for a short period of time. There is nothing like the company of a friend who understands and doesn't try to fix you. Peter knew the senselessness of that.

And so, Peter, I can only share your heart via this book now. Can hope that people grok what you lived so seamlessly. What is that? you might well ask. It is the heart of someone who had entered the Kingdom of Wholeness and found it to be nothing less than beautiful. Something to rest with, something to join hands with. The very core of the heart.

## Touched by the Hand of Sorrow

This light is focused on myself. It wants to heal and hold me in its embrace. It doesn't have human arms or words; it must steal into the brokenness and hold it. All I have to do is know I am fragile and strong at the same time. It has always been that way. We are all that way. No one has it made or can avoid the inevitable. Life is inevitable and so is death.

The tears cannot be kept back. Falling into my lap. Cascading from my fingertips. Washing over my silence. Tending the cracked earth of my emotional desert. What will bloom is because of death touching life and making it live on a higher level. No one wants to go there. No one wants to descend before they ascend and then return to descend again and again.

Life is hard. Death is hard. Love is the gift. If you are touched by the hand of sorrow and draw back, you are just being human. Once you move forward and let it be yours, it lets go. It lets go.

## The Hermit Leaves the Hut: A Little Story about Wholeness

One day the hermit left the hut. It was a time for shedding everything that weighed her down. The first thing she did was cry a million tears. Each tear cut a brighter scene of what was to come. As she stepped out the door, the heavens rejoiced. She heard hosannas and angels murmuring, "The hermit has left the hut. Rejoice!"

She did not look back lest she turn into a pillar of rice cakes and she had never liked those. She kept walking, sodden with tears and light. She did not look back lest she turn into a loaf of stale bread. She feared being nibbled to death by ducks.

The hermit rejoiced at her new-found freedom to speak the truth. She yelled at the sky in feigned madness, "Don't mess with ME!"

She tried out her new voice as she walked along. "Don't tell ME your troubles!" And no one did.

She realized that her sadness was falling off her spirit like wearing one of those microfiber raincoats. In its place was "Don't mess with ME!" And her spirit began to grow.

But at the very end of the day, she shed another tear. This time it felt different. It turned her into an angel of compassion. It said, "You are whole now. You are whole."

And the hermit never went back to the hut. She heard that they turned it into a Starbucks, but that was just hearsay.

Writing a book about the loss of two men dear to me has been hard. Peter entwined his heart with mine—no matter that it was breaking. As I read his words, it breaks again, but this time yielding up its treasure more easily.

I will always have him with me, as I always have Bob. My son and I live this life knowing that the heart is often too full for words. So we have a companionable silence, a sense that the other may be having a rough time. It has not always been this way. For years we kept the war going to keep the grief at bay.

But grief has its lessons to teach. It has made me a writer. Has made me deeper and wiser. I often wish the past could be undone. Don't we all?

One day the director will make his final cut and all that will remain will be the silence.

Somehow I think Peter will be just fine with that.

# The Everyday Entrance to Eternity

*It is morning.*
*I am standing on*
*the map of eternity.*
*I am exactly at the*
*right place*
*at the right time.*


Peter taught me the everyday entrance to eternity. That is, every moment we spend in pure awareness is eternal. The simplest movements made from awareness are love itself.

He played "'Tis the Gift to be Simple" on his little penny whistle as he sat outside in the sun. With his cats, he was the complete package of a happy man. He watched them like they were the best movie he had ever seen.

He wrote lots of people during the time he was confined by his strokes. He helped us all. He repeatedly pointed to simplicity as the great and final teacher for him.

Ultimately, we are led to truth by the tiny amount of it we have inside. If we are serious in our intentions, this investment grows. We, once complex mental creatures living by our wits, are now happy to just live without any expectations.

Our own lives become agents of change for others.

# The Last Message

*Such love does*
*the sky now pour,*
*that whenever I stand in a field,*
*I have to wring out the light,*
*When I get*
*home.*

St. Francis of Assisi

I woke up this morning suffused with love, knowing that if I could express it, that would be a good thing. But it has already vanished, leaving me with just a memory of how good it felt all over my body. Yes, it was like foreplay with divinity. A touching, a reaching into the essence of love, on fire with healing light. I yearned into it, knowing that this love would take me when it saw fit and not a moment sooner. All I can do is wait.

I could not tell you when I received the last message from Peter. It was sometime after Bob had died. My life went on just as Peter said it would. No matter how deep my grief was, the sky was still blue and the grass still green. I had no idea that years later I would be collecting his words so that others could enjoy his experience of awakening.

When my friend David was painting the kitchen last year, I told him about Peter, since David often is in touch with spirits. "He's right here," David said. "He wants you to know that he valued your friendship as much as you valued his." And I smiled.

This little book belongs, not to me or to Peter, but to anyone who feels the vibrancy hidden between the lines. Anyone who puts the book down in order to look up at the wild blue sky. Therein lies the answer to the secret of life.

Vicki

CONSCIOUS.TV is a TV channel which broadcasts on the internet at www.conscious.tv. It also has programmes shown on several satellite and cable channels around the world including the Sky system in the UK where you can watch programmes at 8.30 pm every evening on channel No. 192. The channel aims to stimulate debate, question, enquire, inform, enlighten, encourage and inspire people in the areas of Consciousness, Non-Duality and Science. It also has a section called 'Life Stories' with many fascinating interviews.

There are over 200 interviews to watch including several with communicators on Non-Duality including Richard Bates, Burgs, Billy Doyle, Bob Fergeson, Jeff Foster, Steve Ford, Suzanne Foxton, Gangaji, Greg Goode, Scott Kiloby, Richard Lang, Francis Lucille, Roger Linden, Wayne Liquorman, Jac O'Keefe, Mooji, Catherine Noyce, Tony Parsons, Halina Pytlasinska, Genpo Roshi, Satyananda, Richard Sylvester, Rupert Spira, Florian Schlosser, Mandi Solk, James Swartz, Art Ticknor, Joan Tollifson, and Pamela Wilson. There is also an interview with UG Krishnamurti. Some of these interviewees also have books available from Non-Duality Press.

Do check out the channel as we are interested in your feedback and any ideas you may have for future programmes. Email us at info@conscious.tv with your ideas or if you would like to be on our email newsletter list.

WWW.CONSCIOUS.TV

# Books *from*
# Non-Duality Press

If you enjoyed this book you might be interested in other titles published by Non-Duality Press.

CPSIA information can be obtained at www.ICGtesting.com
Printed in the USA
LVOW06s0846081014

407823LV00005B/424/P